# Pitching for Startups

*11 Strategic Steps to Successfully Speak in Public & Build Your Business*

**Andy O'Sullivan**

**Beatrice**

*To whom I owe it all*

# LEGAL NOTICES

The information presented herein represents the view of the author as of the date of publication. Because of the rate with which conditions change, the author's reserve the right to alter and update his opinion based on the new conditions. This book is for informational purposes only. While every attempt has been made to verify the information provided in this book, neither the authors nor their affiliates/partners assume any responsibility for errors, inaccuracies or omissions. Any slights of people or organizations are unintentional. If advice concerning legal, financial or any other real estate related matters is needed, the services of a fully qualified professional should be sought. This book is not intended for use as a source of legal or accounting advice.

**STATEMENT OF EARNINGS/DISCLAIMER.** Every effort has been made to accurately represent this product and its potential. Examples in these materials are not to be interpreted as a promise or guarantee of earnings. Earning potential is entirely dependent on the person using our product, ideas and techniques. We do not purport this as a "get rich scheme".

Your level of success in attaining the results claimed in our materials depends on the time you devote to the program, ideas and techniques mentioned, your finances, knowledge and various skills. Since these factors differ according to individuals, we cannot guarantee your success or income level. Nor are we responsible for any of your actions.

Materials in our product and our website may contain information that includes or is based upon forward-looking statements. Forward-looking statements give our expectations or forecasts of future events. You can identify these statements by the fact that they do not relate strictly to historical or current facts. They use words such as "anticipate," "estimate," "expect," "project," "intend," "plan," "believe," and other words and terms of similar meaning in connection with a description of potential earnings or financial performance.

**ALL RIGHTS RESERVED.** No part of this book may be reproduced or transmitted in any form whatsoever, electronic, or mechanical, including photocopying, recording, or by any informational storage or retrieval without the expressed written consent of the authors.

© Andy O'Sullivan

If you do not wish to be bound by the above, you may return this book to the publisher for a full refund.

# TABLE OF CONTENTS

| | | |
|---|---|---|
| Introduction | **Who is Andy O'Sullivan** <br> Why You Will Want to Listen. <br> How He Will Save You Pain. | 13 |
| Preface | **Pitch, Presentation or Speech?** <br> Definition of a Pitch. <br> Why and When a Pitch Matters. <br> Your Future Presentations. | 33 |
| CHAPTER 1 | **Preparation** <br> Why You Need Pitching Skills. <br> Where You Pitch. <br> Achieving Success. <br> Clinching The Deal. | 39 |
| CHAPTER 2 | **Psych (Mindset)** <br> Changing Your View. <br> Moving Your Focus. <br> Normality of Nervousness. <br> Disempowering Questions. | 47 |

| CHAPTER 3 | Perception (Attendee Awareness) | 79 |
|---|---|---|

Attendee Research
Why You?
Standing Out to Fit In.
Activity of Your Investor.
Timing Your Pitch.
Knowing Your Numbers.
The Most Important Sentence.

| CHAPTER 4 | Plan (Planning Your Pitch) | 91 |
|---|---|---|

Pitch Strategy and Achieving Your Result.
The Reason For Each and Every Pitch.
Confirming the Data.
Where to Start.
Your Most Important Sentence.

| CHAPTER 5 | Partition (Subdividing Your Pitch) | 105 |
|---|---|---|
| | Separating The Essential Elements. | |
| | The Key Components. | |
| | Selecting Your Structure. | |

| CHAPTER 6 | Puissance (Establishing Credibility) | 117 |
|---|---|---|
| | How to Start. | |
| | Snatching Attention. | |
| | Making a Great First Impression. | |
| | When Your Pitch Starts. | |

| CHAPTER 7 | Potent (A Compelling Close) | 133 |
|---|---|---|
| | Closing For Success. | |
| | Getting Remembered. | |
| | The Serial Position Effect. | |
| | Avoiding the Common Mistakes. | |

| | | |
|---|---|---|
| CHAPTER 8 | Pitch Deck (Vital Pitch Slides) | 143 |

Presenting an Overview.
Selecting the Essential Information.
Knowing the Slides Required.
Formatting for Readability.
Adding Appendices.
Supplying Slides.

| | | |
|---|---|---|
| CHAPTER 9 | Presence (Body Language) | 161 |

Speaking with Presence.
Delivering with Impact.
Focussing Your Mind.
Calming Last Minute Nerves.
How to Approach the Speaking Area.
Maintaining Your Credibility.

Contents

CHAPTER 10  P.R.O.M.P.T  **185**
Presentations
(Speaking On The
Spot).
Answering Questions
Off The Cuff.
Formulating a Clear
Answer.
Finishing Confidently.

CHAPTER 11  **Probe (Fearless**  **201**
**Question & Answers)**
The Questions They
Will Ask.
Maintaining Your
Professionalism.
Restating For Clarity.
When You Just Don't
Know.
Communicating An
Answer.
Your Pitch.

| | |
|---|---|
| About Andy O'Sullivan | 223 |
| Acknowledgements | 227 |
| References | 231 |
| Bibliography | 233 |

# INTRODUCTION

## Who is Andy O'Sullivan... and How You Can Now Benefit From All His Pain, Panic and Practice

You may have noticed that whenever there are young children around, they are always happy to play and perform in public.

They are happy to dance, sing, or play instruments in front of family, friends and neighbours.

They will happily do all these things without any fears or worries about getting embarrassed, looking silly or even being judged.

Then something happens to change us.

Something happens that causes us to change the way we see ourselves. This change now makes us worry about what others will think about us.

This change occurs somewhere between childhood and adulthood. It is a change that steals away all the natural confidence we all had when we were born and enjoyed throughout those early years of life.

Rather than feeling happy, relaxed and even excited to perform in front of others, grabbing every opportunity we could ever find, we are now fearful when standing and speaking.

These feelings of fear, panic and pending doom take over immediately we are faced with the ordeal of having to speak in public.

Just the thought of standing and speaking at a meeting that may be weeks away is enough to fill our bodies with all those feelings of dread and fear.

If the idea of speaking in public now fills us with all these unpleasant feelings, I am sure having to sing or dance in front of other people would for many now be a whole lot worse!

## Introduction

## What Changed?

So what has happened to change things for us?

What is it that has changed us from feeling happy and confident when performing to now having all those negative feelings fill our bodies whenever we are in these situations?

You may have heard of the 'fight or flight response' we have whenever we are placed in a stressful situation, like delivering a pitch.

While this is likely to have played a part in my fear of public speaking, there was another factor that affected how I felt about standing in front of large groups with everyone looking at me.

A big part of my fear and, dare I even say, hatred of speaking in public was all down to my early education.

As I now look back, it is a pity that neither of the schools that I attended ever had a programme where they would help us to develop our communication skills and confidence.

These are the skills so critical to achieving success throughout our professional lives.

If anything, the way the schools operated was totally the opposite.

**Punishment and Embarrassment**

At my schools, public speaking was used as a punishment by many of my teachers.

If the teachers felt you or the class were misbehaving in any way, they would force us to read either our work or, even worse, from a textbook to the whole class.

As a young child, struggling to read in front of the class of thirty or so other children, I would naturally stumble or hesitate over some of the words.

## Introduction

This situation was more likely to occur if the words were new to me or in another language that I was learning at the time.

What was the result?

The whole class would immediately erupt into laughter, sometimes even pointing and making unpleasant comments.

I would be left standing there in front of the entire class feeling embarrassed, upset and very much alone.

Placing a child in this position was not a way to help build their confidence and self-esteem during those early formative years.

It was not the fault of all the other children in my class in the way they behaved towards me.

Nor was it mine when I did the same during their public reading sessions as they too stumbled over their words, sometimes silently standing there, red with embarrassment.

**Haunting Memories**

Throughout my school days, speaking or reading in public therefore became an experience to be feared and one to avoid at all costs.

When I meet up with some of my old school friends, we are still haunted by the experiences of those public reading punishments, decades later.

Does this make my fear of public speaking the fault of my teachers?

They were the ones who made the idea of speaking in public something to be feared, making us individually stand up in front of the whole class and read to everyone.

I used to think it was.

**Reflecting to Forgive**

Now, on reflection, I feel they would never genuinely do anything if they knew the effect it would have on us.

Little did they know the effect these regular humiliations would have on both my classmates and me as we grew up and became adults.

In many of the private schools here in the UK and other education systems around the world, they actively encourage and support public speaking.

Schools will have debating clubs and inter-school contests all aimed at developing their students' speaking skills.

Training in how to communicate and confidently speak in public is something I would love to see in every school, worldwide.

## Adulthood

As a young adult, I would always hate being the centre of attention and therefore would work to ensure it was avoided at all costs.

This hatred had an immense effect on both my career and even whenever I was out socialising.

Many years ago, after starting a trainee job at a new company, I was always invited out for some after work drinks on Fridays.

In the bar with my new colleagues, we would often have other people from the department in which we worked join us.

These were people who I had never met or had only had a very brief conversation with.

Vividly I recall how the thought of having to stand there in front of everyone, with them all looking at me, totally scared me as I asked the straightforward question of what drink they would like.

## Introduction

Standing in front of the group, with them all staring at me, was public speaking and I hated it!

It was something that I wanted to avoid at all costs, so came up with an ingenious plan.

Whenever it came to buying a round of drinks (which I was delighted to do), I would always ask one of my close colleagues to get the drinks in and I would give them the money.

Easy!

On reflection, as I was never seen to buy any drinks, all the other people who joined us for those Friday drinks probably perceived me as being very tight with money.

My colleagues, on the other hand, must have been seen to be very generous.

Either way, getting my colleagues to take the orders and buy the drinks never helped me to overcome my fear of speaking in public.

## Avoidance

Throughout my career, I carried on taking every opportunity possible to avoid being in the same situation of speaking in public.

This avoidance would often mean not participating in meetings where there were many attendees or feeling unable to voice my opinion to any proposals presented, even when I was against them.

## Career Block

The lack of confidence to speak in public would affect my career as changing jobs and attending the inevitable interviews were all part of the process.

## Introduction

It would entail having to sit in the interview with people asking lots of questions while looking at me.

This was scary!

If an interview with one or two people scared me, the idea of a panel type process was entirely out of the question.

The thought of facing an interview panel scared me so much, I would avoid applying for any jobs where this was a known part of the process.

While trying to secure what I felt would be my ideal job, there could be other unexpected hurdles.

Once, having cruised through the interview process for what I felt was the perfect job, I hit a huge hurdle.

The company decided all of the shortlisted candidates would need to deliver a 3 to 5 minute presentation to the members of the department in which they would work if successful in their application.

I could not think of anything worse and immediately withdrew my application for the role.

Facing one or two people in an interview was a terrifying thought for me. The idea of a public presentation was just too much.

**Achieving My Potential**

It was some years later while working for an international bank that my fears of speaking up in public came to a head.

My management always perceived me to be a 'good worker', which I was, but something was missing. I wanted more.

Being ambitious, I naturally wanted to have more success in my career, to get promoted, to have a more substantial salary.

Continually, I kept seeing newer and less experienced colleagues climbing the corporate career ladder ahead of me.

What was it that they were doing to get this success?

**Speaking and Saying Nothing New**

These colleagues were the ones who were always actively participating in meetings.

You would find that they would always have an opinion to share in meetings, especially when senior management were present.

On most occasions, the views and ideas they shared were not even their own!

Sometimes all they would do is just repeat and rephrase what somebody else in the meeting had already stated.

Continually, these were the same people the management liked.

While I stayed in exactly the same role, never moving up the corporate career ladder, my colleagues who spoke up became the people who always got noticed, promoted and rewarded.

It became abundantly clear to me that, no matter how hard you work, no matter what hours you are putting in, working evenings and weekends, to stand any chance of getting success, you have to be seen and heard.

That is when it dawned on me!

I had to improve my communication skills.

## Introduction

**The Journey**

As I started out on what was for me a long and tough journey to becoming a more confident public speaker and presenter, I was continually on the lookout for that 'magic pill'.

The one simple step or strategy that would quickly allow me always to feel confident whenever I needed to speak in public.

In my search for this 'magic pill', I started attending countless courses, workshops and seminars and reading all the books on public speaking that I could find.

There were also all of the online courses, articles and videos which I spent many, many hours devouring over my evenings and weekends.

You can find countless tips, tools and techniques on the internet.

They all seem to promise they will help us become better speakers, to have more confidence, to deal better with all those surprise speaking situations.

To the uninitiated, there is also a lot of, dare I say, 'rubbish' that is said about public speaking.

At best it is worthless, while at the worst, it will damage your confidence and along with it any chance you have of achieving success.

After wasting much time and money being given a false belief of instant confidence, having been taught techniques that are ridiculous, I came to what is an obvious conclusion.

There is no 'magic pill'.

Not one simple technique will give you the confidence and skills to allow you to deal with an awkward question, argumentative client or cope when things go terribly wrong.

## Introduction

It was after this realisation that I began what was to become a long and, at times, painful journey of growth.

A journey that would take me from being filled with panic, days before I was due to deliver a pitch or presentation.

Where I would spend days rehearsing my every word, only to deliver pitches and presentations that were seen as a 'major embarrassment'.

Not my words.

Those were the words of my manager at the time.

The very person that I had always been hoping to impress by speaking in public.

**Not A Natural**

You can probably guess, even as an adult, I was not a 'natural' public speaker, yet today that is precisely what everyone perceives me as being.

When people see me regularly delivering perfect pitches or presentations in large auditoriums, they tell me afterwards that I am a 'natural' and how easy it is for 'people like me'.

Those who see me delivering confident speeches and presentations, even off-the-cuff, have not witnessed or seen the pain and panic that got me into the position where I am today, regularly winning awards and recognition for all my continual achievements.

The journey I have been through over all these years was not pleasant or enjoyable, yet it has taught me a tremendous amount.

It has taught me what works, and most importantly what does not.

It is all this first-hand knowledge and experience that is now available for you in this book.

Lucky you!

# Introduction

You now get the benefit of all the pain, stress and upset that I went through, which will now ensure you become confident and competent as you now successfully create and deliver winning speeches, presentations and pitches with the tips in this book.

Enjoy the journey....

I will be here every step of the way.

*Andy*

**Andy O'Sullivan**

andy@academyofpublicspeakers.com
www.academyofpublicspeakers.com
**LinkedIn:** - http://andy.chat/linkedin
**Twitter:** - http://andy.chat/Twitter
**Facebook:** - http://andy.chat/facebook

# Key Points

## Introduction

*Who is Andy O'Sullivan... and How You Can Now Benefit From All His Pain, Panic and Practice*

In today's business world, you need to be able to speak in public to achieve success.

Public speaking skills are essential to ensure you are able to share your opinions and views.

You need to confidently and competently be able to share your value proposition.

# PREFACE

## Pitch, Presentation or Maybe Even a Speech

*Which Will You Deliver and If It Really Matters to Your Success*

When you are speaking in public, are you giving a pitch, presentation or a speech?

This is one of those questions that often occupies my clients as though they will have to adopt an entirely different method for their creation process.

Some people feel that a speech will only ever be given in a more formal setting such as a wedding, whereas they deliver a pitch to a prospective buyer, client or investor.

After a successful pitch when they have become a client or investor, other people feel they would now only deliver presentations to them.

If this difference between a speech, pitch and presentation is correct, I wonder where the keynote speech that we see delivered at business conferences and events fits into the definition.

Here is what the Oxford Dictionary (2017) gives as its definition of a pitch:

> *A form of words used when trying to persuade someone to buy or accept something.*

To 'persuade someone' is precisely what we are trying to achieve when meeting with buyers or investors.

How then is a presentation different from a pitch?

# Preface

A presentation is what the Oxford Dictionary (2017) defines as: -

> *A speech or talk in which a new product, idea, or piece of work is shown and explained to an audience.*

When we are standing up in front of our team, explaining an idea and asking them to accept it, are we presenting or pitching?

I know from my own experience of the business world that most people will use 'presentation' to describe the act of speaking in public, whether this is to their colleagues or clients.

When they are presenting to achieve an order or investment, the term pitch will instead now be used.

The name we assign to the process is insignificant here.

It is how we go about creating a connection with the people attending the meeting, conveying our ideas and achieving our objectives that are the critical parts and reason for speaking.

It is useful for you to appreciate the similarity as this knowledge will help you as both your skills and business now grow and these terms get used.

While there is no significant difference between the steps required, in this book I will use the term pitch as this is the focus of what we are looking to create and deliver.

Follow along and by the end of this book, you will have all the tips, tools and techniques required to create a compelling, winning pitch.

# **Key Points**

## **Pitch, Presentation or Maybe Even a Speech**

*Which Will You Deliver and If It Really Matters to Your Success*

Whether it is a pitch, presentation or speech, the aims are the same – to convey information.

Your objectives and the success you achieve are what is most important.

This book uses the term pitch, but the skills you will learn will also help you with your future public speaking, whether you feel they are presentations or speech.

# CHAPTER 1

## Preparation

*Why You Now Need Pitching for Startups*

In today's world, we are fortunate to have access to a whole wealth of information that is literally at our fingertips.

On our phone and laptop, we can access information that could only once have been dreamt about.

With access to all this information, I am sure you will have at some time seen some of the limitless number of blog posts, books and videos available as you seek to develop your speaking skills.

Many of these resources will contain valuable information that will be of help to you.

There are also those that offer material which is of, shall we say, a more dubious nature.

It was while reading, watching and learning from all of these resources and the many courses that I had paid good money to attend, that I realised there was not a concise source of information that would give me exactly what it takes to have success in today's world.

Everything I had read and even all of the courses that I attended came from the same position.

The position that I was always going to be speaking from the front of a room with rows of seats in front of me and all those eyes staring back.

While this may be a fair assumption for many other people, it was not always going to be like this for me.

## Preparation

Sure, there were times when this was precisely how I would be delivering my pitch.

There were, however, more occasions when the audience would be a lot smaller and the meeting far more informal.

There were times when I met a potential client in a local coffee shop. While explaining my business, they would interrupt to ask questions, discuss and even disagree with what I had told them.

Whatever the size of my audience, there was a need for me to create and deliver a pitch with confidence and clarity that would stand up to their scrutiny and very detailed questioning.

Yet, I could not find a reputable resource to show me exactly how to deliver these kinds of pitches.

## The Birth of the Startup Success System

Therefore, I had to find out the hard way and experience all the embarrassment that goes with doing it on your own.

This is the reason for taking the time to create the influential Startup Success System™ (evolved from the Corporate Confidence System™), to help with your success when preparing and delivering pitches.

A system that shows you how to: -

>Lose your presentation nerves.

>Feel confident in the moments before speaking in public.

>The correct way to create your pitch.

>How to always impress your potential buyers or investors, even when speaking off the cuff.

This is where the information in this book is going to help you by ensuring you know how to prepare, create and deliver your pitch.

The Startup Success System™ has been taught by me and now used successfully by professionals to grow their businesses.

The core components of the **Startup Success System™** are: -

**Psych -** The importance of approaching your pitch with the right mindset to achieve your success.

**Perception** – How you perceive the people attending the meeting and what you need to know about them to start preparing your pitch.

**Plan** – The purpose of creating your pitch and defining your end result.

**Partition** – Planning your pitch and partitioning it into the essential core elements.

**Puissance** – How to start your pitch with power while snatching everyone's attention.

**Potent** – Ending your pitch with power and how to avoid all the mistakes other professionals make.

**Presentation** – How to create a pitch deck that gets you the desired result.

**Presence** – Speaking with presence and how to deliver your pitch with impact.

**P.R.O.M.P.T Presentations™** – Speaking on the spot and off the cuff with confidence.

**Probe** – Dealing with probing questions and how you can answer any questions with poise and confidence.

As you now learn how to follow and implement each of the components contained in the Startup Success System™, you will see how your skills and abilities skyrocket, allowing you to confidently and successfully deliver your future pitches.

# Key Points

## Preparation

*Why You Now Need Pitching for Startups*

Pitches can be delivered in situations other than when standing up in front of a room.

Client pitches may be delivered in a meeting room, coffee shop or even on the phone.

Discovering how you can create, and confidently deliver, a pitch is critical to your success.

# CHAPTER 2

# Psych

*The Importance of Approaching Your Pitch With The Right Mindset to Achieve Your Success*

When meeting my new clients, I can almost guarantee one of the very first questions they will ask me within ten minutes is how they can get over the anxiety or nerves they feel when having to speak in public or deliver a pitch.

My clients are seeking that one secret to solve what they perceive as their 'problem' when having to deliver a pitch in front of their potential buyers or investors.

What they are all searching for is the 'magic pill' that will instantly take away all of their nerves and fears.

A single action, doctrine or idea that will immediately take them from afraid and apprehensive when thinking about their pitch into a courageous and fearless presenter.

As someone who has spent so much of my time trying to find this very same 'magic pill', I appreciate exactly how they feel and what they want to achieve.

When explaining to them that unfortunately there is not just one simple, easy 'thing' they can do to instantly feel confident before and during the time they are delivering a pitch, they show such a look of disappointment.

It is a bit like telling a child Father Christmas does not exist.

Not that I have ever done that to a child.

I can just imagine how a child would look and feel on hearing the news about Father Christmas.

The journey of growing the confidence to speak and pitch to buyers or investors starts with our mindset.

Our mindset is how we think about what is currently going on around us in our business and what is happening in the days and weeks before our pitch.

It also includes what we perceive might occur in the hours before, during and even after we have finished speaking.

Let us now take a look at some of the concrete steps we can take to feel more confident.

**First Step**

The first step to building your pitching confidence is accepting that there is no one single strategy to remove instantly any fears you may have when speaking in public.

It has been mentioned previously, but this is so important that it is worth reiterating.

Your confidence and the success of your pitch is a combination of altering your mindset and adopting the tips, tools and techniques you will discover in this book.

It is acquiring, learning and practising all of these tips, tools and techniques in this book, that will rapidly help you to complete your journey to becoming a confident public speaker, now being able to pitch with certainty and success.

Putting into action what you learn is the essential part of the process. Resist the temptation to keep waiting for everything to be 'perfect' and to have all the information and skills to start speaking.

There will always be something extra or new to learn.

What you are about to discover in this book is not fluff and theory, it is all based on my personal, and at times, bitter experiences, as I struggled to become the confident professional speaker and entrepreneur that I am today.

**Dating Excitement**

Do you remember the excitement of going on a date?

The build-up in the days before as we prepared where we would go, what we would wear, and maybe even say.

You may have mentally planned how your time together would go.

Then there were the nerves and butterflies before the big moment of the first date.

Unless you are fortunate, it is something we go through many times searching for that one special person.

It is only natural to be nervous before a date as you are eager and excited to see them.

Have you ever noticed how we experience some of the same symptoms as when speaking in public?

The symptoms we have of nerves, apprehension, butterflies, etc.

These are now, however, viewed differently. This time, it can even get referred to as a 'phobia of public speaking'.

It is entirely normal to have some feelings of nervousness in the lead up to any occasion that is important to you, such as a date or delivering a pitch in front of your potential buyers or investors.

It will help if you acknowledge to yourself that these feelings are all perfectly normal.

Everyone has these feelings of nervousness at some time.

Over the years, while running my many courses on public speaking and training entrepreneurs to create and deliver winning pitches, I have asked the attendees to share some of the symptoms they feel in the days or hours leading up to their pitch.

The most frequent ones are: -

>Sweaty palms.
>
>Dry mouth.
>
>Pounding heart.
>
>Sweating.
>
>Butterflies in stomach.

Do any of these sound familiar to you?

What physical symptoms do you feel leading up to speaking in public or delivering a pitch?

One fascinating revelation always comes out of this sharing.

Those attending my courses start to realise how they are not the only ones to feel nervous or experience these symptoms.

We all do.

**Is it Only Me?**

Long before I became a multi-award winning speaker, whenever I used to attend meetings, I would always sit there wondering why all the other speakers were so confident and relaxed, whereas I was feeling so nervous.

What was it they knew or were doing differently to me?

In truth, all the other speakers will also have been feeling some public speaking anxiety, even if they would not admit to it.

It is not just professionals who experience nervousness and anxiety before delivering a pitch.

Many professional musicians and actors have admitted to experiencing stage fright.

Sometimes it is so severe it gets to the point that they are physically ill and throw up before their performance.

A few well-known artists who experience this level of stage fright are Adele, Rhianna and Katy Perry.

In a way, we should take some comfort from the thought that if these highly talented and accomplished artists experience anxiety before their performances, we as the occasional presenter are no different.

## The Signs

As my skills and experience grew, I started to recognise the signs of nervousness in all the other speakers who I had previously viewed as confident communicators.

That was when I realised it was not just me.

I have often seen entrepreneurs sitting in a meeting, literally rewriting their pitch notes in the moments before they were due to present as they let the stress and pressure build up inside of them.

Somehow they suddenly started to feel the new ideas that had come to mind at the highest moment of anxiety were going to be better than all those they would have prepared and practiced before the meeting.

Really?

Changing any part of a pitch in the minutes before it is due to be delivered is the worst time to consider altering what you have planned to say.

How do I know this?

It is something that I have also done, leading to disastrous pitches.

There are a few reasons for making changes to come over as more spontaneous, but these are different to rapidly rewriting whole parts of a pitch.

## Acceptance

We now know that all of the entrepreneurs and speakers you will have seen presenting will have at some time felt some nerves before delivering a pitch, even if they look so calm, confident and professional.

## It is perfectly normal.

Knowing that it was not just me who felt nervous about speaking in public made a big difference to my confidence, as it turned out that I was not unusual!

I know it is obvious, but so often we can get trapped into believing we are the only ones who feel like this. We are all human, so have the same feelings, admittedly in different quantities.

## Power of Our Imagination

While any feelings of nervousness may be normal, one of the things they may do is make us imagine the worst of all possible scenarios.

Can you picture this: -

You have a pitch to deliver at a meeting in 3 weeks.

Naturally, you know the business and are therefore very qualified to deliver the pitch.

How do you feel in the weeks, days, hours and even minutes leading up to the pitch?

I used to feel scared witless!

Even the thought of delivering a pitch that may still have been weeks away would set off many different feelings of sheer panic.

The physical sense of stress and anxiety would only increase as the day and time for my pitch drew even closer.

Why is it that we can sometimes show symptoms way in advance of our speaking event?

An event that may still be weeks away.

**What If....?**

Let us take a step back and look at the thought process that I went through as soon as I had agreed to deliver a pitch or come to that, just to speak in public at any size meeting.

If you are like me, in the run-up to giving a pitch, you will be asking yourself a series of 'what if' questions.

Questions like: -

> What if I look silly?
>
> What if I forget my words?
>
> What if they don't like me?
>
> What if they hate my idea?
>
> What if they know more than me?
>
> What if they challenge my figures?
>
> What if I don't know the answer to a question?

Maybe you are asking questions like these?

These questions would continually be spinning round and round in my head, even in my dreams.

All this was doing over time was adding to all the stress and tension that I felt and was not serving or helping me in any way.

As you now look at the list of questions that I was continually asking myself, do you see what they all have in common?

There is one clear theme to all of the questions.

Every single one of these questions was about me.

Yes, me!

The whole focus of every question is what is going to happen to me at the event and how everyone who will be attending is going to perceive me.

While this is the natural approach to start taking in the lead up to any pitch, it is entirely the wrong strategy to have running in a continual cycle through your mind.

So how do we stop running this cycle of all these 'what if' questions in the days before our pitch?

The answer is simply - Stop being so selfish.

There I said it....

Stop being so selfish!

I do not mean to be harsh, but it is so important to get this point.

A critical first step in reducing our public speaking nerves in the lead up to a pitch is to change where we focus.

Let us look at it this way.

Imagine this situation: -

You have invited some friends over to your home for a small party next week.

What would be your thought process?

Stop and take a moment to think about it.

I am sure you would start off by thinking about what food and drinks you should buy in to cater to their individual tastes.

Maybe to ensure all of your friends have a wonderful time you may need to have prepared a mix of meat, vegetarian, vegan, or gluten-free foods for them.

Were all your thoughts all about how you can ensure that you are going to have an awesome time and what the guests can do to ensure you enjoy the evening?

Do you ask questions such as: -

    What if I get bored?

    What if I don't fancy pudding?

    What if I don't enjoy the party?

    What if I don't enjoy the conversation?

I am sure these would not be the very first questions that spring to mind or ones that you keep worrying about before your party.

## Altering Our Focus

Just as a good host takes the time to ensure all of their guests will have a good time at their event, so you can now start to focus on those who will be listening to your pitch.

Instead of having the mental focus 100% internally on us, worried about how people are going to perceive us, start to now think about all those who will be attending the meeting.

What can you do to ensure they all enjoy listening to you, are interested in your business and ultimately want to buy or invest?

When you start to change your focus away from all of your internal thoughts and instead out and onto the buyers or investors attending, any symptoms of public speaking stress will soon begin diminishing.

Even if you stop reading now and never see another word in this book, following this single strategy will make you feel more confident and less stressed when pitching for your business.

## Attendees

As you saw in the list of 'what if' questions listed above, I used to get quite stressed worrying about how everyone attending the event was going to behave and perceive me.

My own experiences, and those of all my coaching clients, have shown me that these break down into two common ways for imagining how the pitch will go.

The first is imagining that everyone attending the meeting at which you are going to be pitching will immediately start to act like a flock of vultures.

They will all sit there, waiting for the first opportunity to tear into both you and your business.

Then once they start, it then continues all through your pitch.

They will deliberately ask you loads of really awkward and tough questions that they already know you are going to be unable to answer.

Maybe they will even argue with you or tell you that you are totally wrong.

Either way, they will leave you and your reputation torn to shreds in front of everyone.

That is so scary!

If you have any thoughts like these, well no wonder you felt nervous about speaking in public.

An unfriendly audience was one of my biggest worries when it came to delivering any pitch, especially if I thought they might know more than me in this area of the business.

In truth, it is utter rubbish.

When was the last time you attended any meeting having already decided to attack one of the speakers?

Have you ever decided or arranged in advance to gang up with everyone attending a meeting so you can all tear into the speaker's presentation or pitch?

To deliberately humiliate them in front of everybody who happens to be attending?

To utterly destroy their reputation and their business?

I am sure the answer to all these questions will be no, never.

The same applies to everybody who is attending the event at which you are pitching.

You may find that the potential buyer or investors in the meetings at which you are speaking will disagree, debate or just ignore what you have proposed.

They may ask challenging questions or say thank you, but no thank you for your proposal.

That's ok!

You are never going to have everyone agreeing with you or falling in love with your business all of the time.

What you will find is that in most meetings where you will be presenting and pitching, is that everyone will be well-behaved asking appropriate and professional questions.

Always think of those attending your pitch as intelligent, respectful listeners.

## Disaster Strikes....

The second way of imagining how the pitch will go is to see everything going horribly wrong.

As mentioned previously with the 'what if' questions, your mind will start to imagine what will happen if no one turns up, you forget your words, you look silly, or maybe unable to answer one of their questions.

It is incredible how the mind can make it seem so real, isn't it?

As I used to run these questions and thoughts through my mind, I would get palpitations weeks in advance of my pitch.

## A Change of View

A far more positive and powerful way to use your imagination is to see everything going well for you.

Many professional sports stars use a process of positive visualisation before their game or event.

With this technique, you visualise your incredible success and how you can see everyone smiling, nodding and engrossed as you deliver your pitch.

Hear all the enthusiastic applause as you finish and feel those 'pats on the back' for a pitch well delivered from your team.

This technique helped me whenever I used to feel stressed at the thought of speaking at an event at which only 8 people were attending.

I would visualise giving the speech in a stadium of 80,000 and a worldwide television audience.

After doing this visualisation a few times, when I then thought about speaking in front of 8 people, the fear had dramatically reduced.

In my mind, I had given the speech successfully in front of 80,000, so now 8 investors seemed nothing in comparison.

Get into the habit of keeping all the thoughts you have about your forthcoming pitch positive.

Stop yourself whenever an imagined worry or negative thought pops into your mind and become a focus.

I know this is easier said than done, particularly in the beginning, but with practice, it will become a lot more straightforward for you.

**Preparing and Practicing**

Let us cover briefly here writing and practicing your pitch as this can reduce your speaking nerves when done correctly.

We will cover this subject in far more detail in later chapters.

We can all sometimes procrastinate about getting tasks completed which we would really rather not undertake.

In years gone by, I have been guilty of preparing my presentations and pitches a few hours before the meeting, convincing myself that I was just too busy to dedicate any time to making the slides or writing my notes.

All this did was increase the mental pressure that I felt sitting in the meeting, waiting for my turn to speak.

My pitch would have been another stressful situation simply because I had not taken the time to prepare and practice.

Do not let creating your pitch be a task that you procrastinate over or leave to the last moment.

When you allow yourself plenty of time to adequately prepare and practice your pitch, you will feel far more confident when it comes to delivering it in front of those important potential buyers or investors.

## We Can Not Control Everything

Another source of stress is what to do if things actually do go wrong.

There are always going to be certain things and events outside of your control.

For example, you are unable to stop the fire alarm activating or an important investor being delayed by a previous meeting.

As you have no control over these types of events, there is little point in worrying about them happening or adding to the pressure you may be feeling, as it just makes you feel more nervous.

It is always worthwhile adequately preparing for any eventualities that are within your control.

For example, printing your notes and pitch deck in case the laptop stops working or having a copy saved to a USB flash drive that you can take to the meeting.

Having prepared for these eventualities, you can now stop worrying about them occurring.

Once you have completed this book, you will find there is a combination of techniques to ensure you feel confident creating and delivering your next pitch.

## Venue

When you arrive in the meeting room or venue at which you are going to be delivering your pitch, there is one action you can take that will help settle any nerves you are feeling.

Walk to the speaking area, stand there and look out at the empty seats.

Get a feeling and sense of what it will be like when you are standing there delivering your pitch.

Look around the room and imagine all the seats filled with supportive listeners, eager to buy or invest.

You may feel it is helpful to perform all or some of your presentation out loud as this will give a sense of the volume level you will need to speak at during your pitch.

There is no reason to feel any embarrassment about delivering your pitch while a few people in the room are pottering about or helping with the setup.

There are likely to be far more people in the room listening to you later, so grab the opportunity.

As everyone arrives in the meeting room, take the time to stand casually for a moment in the speaking area, looking out as everyone takes their seats.

There is no need to feel self-conscious doing this as no one will take any notice of you.

When it comes to the actual pitch, you will have already seen where everyone will be sitting and heard your voice. It will now feel a lot less stressful for you.

These steps will help you to feel more relaxed during your pitch and are going to be covered in more detail throughout the book.

In later chapters, we are going to cover preparing and presenting your pitch.

.

# Key Points

## Psych

*The Importance of Approaching Your Pitch With The Right Mindset to Achieve Your Success*

There is no "magic pill" to remove the anxiety of speaking in public.

Some feelings of nervousness are perfectly normal.

All other speakers will have felt some anxiety when pitching.

Avoid continually asking 'what if' questions in the run-up to your pitch.

Act as an excellent host and focus on what you can do for the listeners.

Always imagine everything going well.

Arrive in the room early and then take the time to stand in the speaking area.

# CHAPTER 3

## Perception

*How You Perceive The People Attending The Meeting and What You Need to Know About Them to Start Preparing Your Pitch*

When you have a date set for delivering the pitch, you may feel excited, worried or even scared.

That is how I used to feel!

These are of course entirely natural feelings to have and are experienced by most people.

## Questions and Ideas

With the idea of the pitch in your mind, you will probably start giving some thought to the critical areas you will need to cover.

Typically, many ideas will start running through your head of the concepts, data or information that you can include and share with everyone attending.

## Research

A large part of your initial pitch preparation will be the research on who will be attending the meeting at which you will be speaking and maybe also their company.

Researching the company will help you to show during the pitch how your business, product or service is a perfect fit for them.

This information is essential in ensuring that the pitch you create will engage and excite everyone attending, while giving them all of the vital information that they will need to receive.

Taking the time at this stage to conduct detailed research on those attending and their company will be critical to the success you achieve with your pitch.

## Follow the Steps

The following is the sequence of steps to take in advance of your pitch to compile your research.

## Step 1

The first area to look at is who will be attending the meeting at which you will be delivering your pitch. Some of the attendees' areas you may like to look at are: -

## Buyers

When you are pitching to buyers, look to see how your: -

**Product suits the selection of similar merchandise currently stocked.**

>The retailer will need to be already selling similar merchandise for them to be interested in purchasing your product.
>
>A shop that specialises in sportswear will have little interest in stocking a revolutionary new kitchen appliance.

Perception

**Product fits into the price band for their regular customer base.**

Retailers will have their brand focussed on different segments of the same market.

These range from the affluent to the price conscious consumer.

A kitchen appliance retailing for $100 may be too cheap for some stores to stock or too expensive for others.

**Product will stand out from the similar merchandise stocked.**

What is it about your product that will make it stand out on the shelves if stocked by the retailer?

Will it be its design, features or price?

**Product compares to the similar merchandise stocked.**

As an entrepreneur, it is essential to know of other companies operating on the market and offering similar products.

Be prepared to compare and contrast why your product is superior, unique or provides something unparalleled to anything else on the market or currently stocked by the retailer.

## Investors

When you are pitching to receive financing from investors, some of the information you may look to discover to help you achieve your objective is: -

Have they invested in similar industries?

What have been their most recent investments?

Do they have a personal background in your industry?

Do any of your connections have any experience of working with the investors?

Do they have any existing knowledge or understanding of the business which you are pitching?

## Step 2

Can you imagine how you would feel turning up to a meeting expecting 1 person to be attending to hear your pitch and seeing 10 sitting there?

The number attending the meeting will have an influence on how you structure and deliver your pitch.

Enough copies of any documents and handouts will be required and printed for everyone attending.

It will give a very unprofessional impression if you ask buyers or investors to share copies of your pitch documents, all because you did not take the time to check on the number of people attending.

## Step 3

The final step is to ask how long you will have in the meeting to deliver your pitch and take questions.

Once you have a time slot, stick to it.

Many entrepreneurs somehow feel their business, and the opportunity they are offering is so incredible, that they will speak for longer than the time they have been allocated.

In truth, neither the buyers or investors will appreciate you going over the time that they allowed to see you and hear the pitch for your business.

Always finish within the time you have been allocated.

# Key Points

## Perception

*How You Perceive The People Attending The Meeting and What You Need to Know About Them to Start Preparing Your Pitch*

Take the time to research who will be attending the meeting as this is critical to the success of your pitch.

When pitching to buyers, look to see how your product will fit into their current range in terms of similarity with existing stock and price bands.

## Perception

To help with your chance of receiving investment, aim to discover if the investor has a background in your industry or a history of making similar investments.

Discover if the investor is currently active or is known to any of your connections.

# CHAPTER 4

## Plan

*The Purpose of Creating Your Pitch, a Single Strategy & Your End Result*

Where ever you are currently in the development of your business, the ability to communicate precisely in the pitches you deliver to buyers or investors will have an immense impact on the success you achieve.

Depending on your audience, some of what they will be interested in hearing from you can be: -

>Who you are.
>
>What you do.
>
>Your target market.
>
>Scalability of business.
>
>Plans for profit and growth.
>
>Evaluation of market demand.

While working with clients building their businesses, I have had the pleasure of seeing some incredible pitches delivered by people working in different industries offering a massive variety of opportunities to investors, distributors and retailers.

These were the successful speakers who had clearly researched the people attending the meeting and listening to their pitch.

The result?

Those speakers connected and engaged with everyone in the room so well, we were all intrigued and interested in both their business and the plans they were sharing.

These speakers received the interest or investment they were seeking.

Then there were all the other speakers.

**Losing Credibility**

These were the ones who had not taken the time to prepare or even update the slides in their pitches.

Some speakers I saw had merely just dusted off an old pitch they had created sometime earlier.

Sitting through their pitches, I used to wonder if they had even seen the slides before as they had a look of surprise at some of the information displayed on the screen.

A speaker delivering a pitch at one meeting I was attending showed us a slide on which the font selected for his data was so small, it was impossible to read.

That was from the front row.

The speaker then admitted his data had been added to the slides some time ago.

It was sloppy for that speaker not to have updated the financial projections he was presenting for investment.

Then it got even worse.

While the speaker may have admitted he had added the financial figures months ago, it turned out that data was itself even older.

The figures on the slide he was showing were so out of date, it was of no relevance to anyone in the room or the investment he was seeking.

Although the speaker carefully went through the figures on that single slide, it was a waste of everyone's time.

This information was on one of the first slides in his pitch, so can you guess what we were all sitting there wondering?

We were all wondering if the figures on the first slide were out of date and so could not be trusted, what about the rest of his pitch?

Could we believe anything he was presenting to us?

That day, the speaker struggled to answer the few questions he was asked and, not surprisingly, failed to win any investment.

It is essential to create the slides in your pitch deck so they contain the most up-to-date information available to you.

It is okay to reuse slides, they just need to be updated or adjusted to suit your audience.

We will cover creating your pitch deck later in this book.

## Purpose

There can only ever be a single purpose for creating and delivering a pitch.

What is it?

Are you looking to receive an investment in your business or sell your product, service or solution?

## Writing Your Pitch

The point at which you sit down to write your pitch is the one that I used to find the most challenging.

I would structure writing my pitch by deciding in advance that say, on Monday at 1pm, I was going to sit down to write it out in full.

At the given time with the laptop open, I would sit there ready to type out my masterpiece.

It took me a very long time to realise it, but this is the wrong way ever to go about creating a pitch.

I would always find that I did not know what the key message was that I wanted to convey in my pitch to get the interest and investment.

Instead of typing away, I would often just sit looking at my blank document, with a feeling of frustration growing inside.

The pressure would then build as I would have to produce something, especially when up against a tight deadline.

On the occasions where I had left creating the pitch until the morning of the meeting, I would undoubtedly feel the pressure.

At times, this internal pressure became so intense, it made clear, logical thought impossible as it verged on a feeling of panic.

It took me quite a while to realise that the process of creating a compelling pitch that impacts on your listeners is not the same as writing an email.

The process that I had been using for years was to start at the beginning with my opening introductory comments and slowly work through to what was going to be my close.

This way of writing was not an efficient way to spend my time creating a pitch.

Another method I had seen used and tried was to start with creating my pitch deck, then write the content around it.

The trouble with all these methods?

With each of these methods, we start at the beginning, working towards the end.

While this may seem to be entirely logical (it did to me), these methods will never allow you to create a pitch that connects and excites your potential investors or buyers.

Knowing how to create and deliver a well-structured pitch that will interest the investor or buyer will have an immense impact on the success you achieve with receiving the desired investment or order.

## Planning Your Route

The way to connect with and excite the investors or buyers is to take them on a journey as you progress through your pitch.

When we plan any journey, there are three things we need to know: -

>Where we are going.
>
>Where we are starting from.
>
>The route to take.

We will have more success when, to quote Stephen Covey (2004), we 'begin with the end in mind'.

## End Result

Just like when starting any journey, you will need to know the end before setting off, that way you will know when you have arrived.

We need first to know what it is we are looking to achieve from our pitch and the journey we are going to embark on with our investors and buyers.

You may establish that your end result will be: -

- An investment of $x in exchange for a maximum y% equity.

- An order for x thousand units delivered in y months for $z.

If you can state the end result of your pitch in a single sentence, then you will have created a very clearly defined destination for your listeners.

With this single sentence written, only the information required to help our listeners reach this destination will need to be added to the pitch.

It is easy to feel that everything we know about the business and market needs to be included, just in case it helps.

In practice, it will often overwhelm those attending.

As you start creating the pitch, anything that does not entice those listening towards your end result and helps generate interest in either placing an order or investing can be discarded.

Be strict with yourself by including what will help you to explain, expand or emphasise the end result you are pursuing.

# Key Points

## Plan

*The Purpose of Creating Your Pitch, a Single Strategy & Your End Result*

There is only one purpose for creating a pitch which is to receive investment in your business or an order for your product/service.

Ensure you maintain credibility by checking that your pitch deck contains the most up-to-date information available.

Before you start creating your pitch, decide and define your end result.

Plan

Write out your end result in a single short sentence.

Include in your pitch only the details that will help you to explain, expand or emphasise the end result.

# Pitching for Startups

# CHAPTER 5

## Partition

*Planning Your Pitch and Partitioning it into The Core Essential Elements to Guarantee Your Success.*

The pitches you create and deliver will have different purposes for why they are being designed and delivered.

They will however all require the same essential elements.

Most other people consider these components to be the: -

    Opening

    Content

    Closing

The order listed above may be the logical flow to follow when creating your pitch, but there is a far more productive way for you to set about creating these components.

The key components of every pitch and the order in which to create them are: -

    End Result

    Body & Transitions

    Closing

    Opening

## 1) End Result

In the previous chapter, we covered how before starting to create your pitch, it is best for you to have defined the end result you are aiming to achieve.

The end result of your pitch is likely to be receiving interest in either placing an order for your product/service or the possibility of an investment in your business.

Creating a single sentence that states your end result is what will contribute to you designing a pitch that achieves your primary objective.

All of the analysis, data and examples will only then be included in your pitch if they help you with achieving the objective set out in your end result.

Be very strict with yourself on this.

Although it may be an interesting fact or story for you to tell, it will only create confusion if it is included and does not help guide the listeners towards your end result.

## 2) Body

With your end result established and created, the second step is to start designing the structure for your pitch.

The structure designing begins with the body.

## Step 1

A super simple way to start is by compiling a list of all the points you need to cover to reach the end result you have created.

List down any thoughts that come to mind without taking any time to consider or filter them out at this stage.

You may find writing the list by hand is more efficient at allowing you to be more creative with your thoughts.

## Step 2

Now that you have created your list, it is time to review and discard any points that do not contribute to the end result of your pitch.

They may be exciting or entertaining, but unless they help to explain or reinforce the message and lead to the end result, take them out.

## Step 3

As you review your list, see if there is a natural or obvious way that it can be structured or segmented. There are many different ways for this to be achieved.

The primary structures that I have found useful are:

*Order*

Here you would either start with the most important moving to the least important or the other way around.

*Logical*

When one idea has a logical flow.

As an example, a pitch on a new product could cover how you came up with the idea, the analysis completed, design and development, testing and the hurdles you have overcome.

*Cause-Effect*

You will use this structure when there is a clear cause of the issue, and you can then show the effect the cause will have or is having.

## Sequence

When there is a connection between a series of events that create a precise sequence, this is the structure to use.

As an example, if you were pitching on a new sales order system, you might cover how the software tracks an order from the moment it has been placed, dispatched and delivered.

## Problem-Solution

Here you would explain the problem, why it happened or occurs, its consequences, and then reveal the solution you are able to provide.

## Pendulum

With this structure, as you present the point, take it to extremes on both sides of the discussion, before you propose a solution that settles in the mid-point.

*Location*

This structure is useful when there is a clear location-based structure for the pitch content.

## Step 4

With the list of all the points you need to cover in the pitch now arranged into a structure to suit your subject, select a single keyword that summarises each section you have created.

This keyword will later become the heading used when creating the slides and notes for the pitch.

## Step 5

You will now have your pitch split into sections, with a keyword that encapsulates each one.

Now is the time to write out in more detail the main point each of the sections will cover.

Support this main point using anecdotes, case studies, financial data, statistics and stories that will help your listeners with their understanding.

## 3) Closing

The closing is your opportunity to reinforce your main message, the takeaway points, and to ask for an order or investment.

## 4) Opening

Create one that captures everyone's attention and answers all the questions they will have in their mind at that time.

The closing and opening are covered in more detail later in the following 2 chapters.

# Key Points

## Partition

*Planning Your Pitch and Partitioning it into The Core Essential Elements to Guarantee Your Success.*

Knowing the key components of every speech and the order in which to create your speech.

Every speech you create requires the same essential elements: -

    1) End Result
    2) Body & Transitions
    3) Closing
    4) Opening
    5) Title

Know the end result before moving on to create the other elements.

All of the analysis, data and examples will only need to be included in your pitch if they help you with achieving the objective set out in your end result.

Select the most appropriate structure for organising the body of your pitch.

# CHAPTER 6

## Puissance

*Starting Your Pitch with Power & Snatching Attention*

You may have heard the saying that you get one chance to make a great first impression.

That saying is definitely true when it comes to delivering something that is so important as your pitch.

Let me ask you a question.

When does a pitch start?

Think about that for a moment as it is not a trick question.

Does it start as you begin speaking?

Maybe while you are being introduced?

How about as you stand up or maybe while walking to the speaking area?

Each of these points will, of course, have an impact on the impression that you make on everyone who is attending and listening to you.

That is the purpose of your pitch - to have left a significant impression on those listening to you.

The impression you create will have started long before your pitch.

Your pitch starts from the very moment you are visible to those attending the meeting.

Recently I was reading some research that showed a candidate's chances of success when attending a job interview can be affected by the first 12 words they say.

The study (Rodionova, 2016) found that interviewers will judge candidates by the quality of their small talk as they are walking to the room where the interview is being held.

In the same way that interviewers are judging candidates before the formal interview has started, you will find that attendees at the meeting will also be judging you and forming an impression before you even begin to deliver your carefully prepared pitch.

Let us suppose you are giving a pitch at the offices of a prospective investor.

As the client arrives in the lobby to meet you, she sees you being rude to the receptionist.

This initial impression you have created will stay in her mind the whole time and will probably be a more prominent memory of you than the content of your pitch.

Do you think the investor will be more or less likely to now invest in your business?

You are creating an impression in people's minds from the moment that you are first in view, so make it a positive one.

## Creating a Captivating Opening

Once you have created the body content, it is time to create an opening that encapsulates the core of your pitch.

The opening of your pitch is the first sentence that is different, exciting and relevant to your business and the attendees.

Create an opening that catches the attendees' attention quickly, builds rapport, and draws them away from other distractions like their smartphones and self-talk.

Other business professionals often have boring, lacklustre openings that are the same as everybody else's, so people soon start to switch off.

Once you have lost the attention of the buyer or investor, it takes hard work and passion winning them back, along with that order or investment.

You can see why your initial sentence is important and integral to ensure you stand out from all the other people who may be pitching that day.

## Ways to Open Your Pitch

Your pitch will need to be started so that it immediately commands the attention of the attendees and gets them interested in hearing more from you.

Here are some suggestions on how you may consider opening: -

## Demonstration

When your pitch is based on a physical product, opening with a short demonstration may do more to show the opportunity you are presenting than an explanation could.

If your product was a new shatterproof glass, 'accidently' dropping it as you start your pitch would certainly get everyone's attention.

## Ask a question

Have you noticed how you will always answer any question that you have been asked?

Even if you just answer it silently?

That is the power of a question.

It will have everyone listening and taking part in your pitch, even if it is a silent part.

Any question you ask must matter to your listeners and have some significance to them otherwise, why should they care or listen to you?

If the question asked is not of interest, they will decide this pitch is not for them and quickly start to switch off.

When the question you ask relates to a subject that is of interest to those attending, they will want to hear more from you and focus on your pitch.

## Ask a Rhetorical Question

When asking a rhetorical question, it will be similar to the point above. The question will need to be one that matters to everyone attending the meeting.

There is one significant advantage of asking a rhetorical question when you are feeling nervous.

You do not have to worry about whether or not anyone answers the question.

It is rhetorical after all!

If they do, well that is great as it shows engagement. On the other hand, as you are not expecting an answer, the silence will not affect your flow.

You will need to give time for people to consider the question in their minds, so pause long enough for them to formulate an answer.

The time it takes the attendees to answer will depend on the question you have asked and how long they will need to consider their reply.

As a guide on the amount of time to allow for the attendees to formulate an answer, mentally respond to the question posed before continuing with your pitch.

## Statistics that surprise

While we can feel any statistics should come later in our pitch, you can grab attention by starting with one that will surprise and interest your listeners.

Here is an example of one statistic that surprised me: -

*1 in 6 women would rather be blind than fat
(Realbuzz, 2012)*

This surprising statistic may be perfect if you are pitching a business, product or service related to the health sector, but would have attendees confused if you were selling lampshades.

As when asking a question, find a statistic from a reliable source that is relevant to your pitch and of interest to those attending.

## Stories

We may not even realise it, but as adults, we all still love to hear stories.

As children, we were captivated when an adult would utter those special words 'once upon a time...'.

We all knew this was now the time to settle down and pay close attention.

In a pitch, it is highly unlikely that we would ever want to start off with 'once upon a time'.

We can still begin with and include stories that are either personal to us or those that will connect with those attending the pitch.

We all can connect quickly with stories that are about people, especially when we personally know or feel for them.

Include appropriate stories from colleagues, celebrities or clients as these are the ones that add interest and impact.

People stories create a stronger and deeper connection with your listeners than talking about concepts, statistics, gadgets or gizmos.

## Quotations

Starting your pitch with an appropriate quote can be a compelling way to get attention.

When selecting the quote for your pitch, look to have one that will resonate with the buyers or investors attending the meeting.

This personalisation will help the buyers or investors to feel that you are talking just to them.

There are many famous quotes that we have all heard hundreds of times.

In fact, we know them so well, we could probably finish them off for the speaker.

These are the kind of famous quotes that you will want to avoid when opening your pitch.

Take the time to find quotes that those attending the meeting are unlikely to have heard before.

The quotes you select can come from many diverse sources.

I suggest not merely searching the web for "quotes" to include in your pitch.

Try to be different and look closer to home, for example, from your parents, siblings, neighbours, in fact, anyone!

When you find an appropriate unknown quote, it will have more impact on those attending the meeting.

Creating a customised opening for your pitch based on your research of who will be attending the meeting, will help you to stand out and have more success.

# Key Points

## Puissance

*Starting Your Pitch with Power & Snatching Attention*

You only get one chance to make a great first impression.

Your pitch starts from the very moment you are visible to those attending. This is the point when you begin to create an impression.

Start your pitch so that it immediately commands the attention of your audience.

Create an opening that will be different to all the other people the buyers & investors will see pitching to them that day.

Select an opening that will resonate with the buyers or investors attending the meeting.

Pitching for Startups

# CHAPTER 7

## Potent

*Ending Your Pitch with Power & Avoiding the Mistakes Other Speakers Make*

We all have a tendency to recall the first and last items in a series best, and the middle items worst.

This recall is what is known as the Serial Position Effect (Indiana.edu, 2016).

This effect also impacts how well we are able to recall the content of a pitch after it has been delivered and we have left the room.

As previously covered, careful thought has to be given to the opening of a pitch to connect and engage with everyone attending the meeting, especially the buyers or investors.

The opening is one part of your pitch that people attending will more clearly recall.

The other part based on the serial position effect is the closing.

The last words of a pitch are just as crucial as the first.

These words require careful consideration to ensure they have the desired impact on your audience long after your meeting has finished.

Before we cover some robust methods for closing a pitch that will ensure everyone remembers your content, let us look at some of the more common errors other speakers make.

These mistakes will confuse the purpose of the pitch and everyone who is listening to them.

The result of this confusion will be a pitch that is soon forgotten.

## New Content

Adding new content when reaching the end of your pitch is a sure fire way to cause confusion in the minds of the listeners.

This new content may be material that the speaker intended to cover earlier but had merely forgotten.

It may also be additional content that the speaker has thought of after a question or point has been raised by someone in the meeting.

When additional content is added that the speaker does not have time to explain, it is likely to lead to confusion in the listener's mind rather than help as the speaker intended.

## Rambling & Waffling

I am sure you will have seen a speaker finish their pitch and then waffle on saying nothing.

Reaching the end of their pitch, they say something like: -

*"So….err…. that's kind of it…really….err….I'd like to thank you all for listening to me…. and for your….err…time…*

This way of closing is by far the most disappointing and forgettable way to close what may have been a perfect pitch.

## Closing with Impact

Now that we know exactly how not to close our pitch, let us see how to close with an impact so that we are always the speaker who will be remembered.

When delivering a pitch, recognise there will often be other business people pitching to the buyers or investors on the same day, maybe even at the same event.

How effectively you close your pitch will be critical to ensuring that everyone will be able to recall what you have covered and the key points.

There are several ways to close a pitch that will capture the attendee's attention, creating a long-lasting impact on them.

Once you have learned the methods of closing a pitch, you will be able to select the one that will work best for you, the occasion and the people to whom you are pitching.

## 1) Personal Story

A personal story will always have the most impact on those listening to you, especially if you are able to show how your proposition has or will affect someone's life.

The story you share may well be based on one of your personal experiences.

There are other sources for your story, with it coming from one of your colleagues, clients or customers.

A story of how your business, product or service has impacted on them will bring the pitch to life as people will easily relate to it.

If you are identifying people while telling the story, be sure to have their permission first.

It will be an untimely end to your pitch if they are sitting and squirming in their seat with embarrassment.

## 2) Read an Email

If you have received an email from a customer or a person influential in your business that endorses the proposal in your pitch, this can be very effective.

The person writing the email which you will read out can say things about your company, proposal, product, service or idea that you would never be able to say to the same effect.

Unless the email has been sent to you as a testimonial, seek their permission to include it in your pitch.

When closing the pitch, we can also use some of the same ideas covered when creating the opening.

## 3) Restate Your Opening

Restating your opening sentences and then reiterating the key points as your close, can be a beneficial way to reinforcing the essence of your pitch.

### 4) Repeat Your Opening

If a rhetorical question was used to open your pitch, it might also be suitable for it to be repeated as the closing sentence.

### 5) Quotations

The unusual or unheard quote that you are planning on using for your opening sentence may also be suitable to use for your final words.

When you reach the conclusion of your pitch simply repeat the quote.

## Selecting the Best

Which of these closings will work best for your pitch, depends on the subject, the message and the end result you defined at the first stage in this process.

You may well find that you use alternative closings for the same pitch when it is being delivered to a different audience.

The one critical thing to include in your closing is to summarise and repeat what it is you are looking to receive such as an order or investment.

As with the opening of your pitch, choose the closing which will most effectively help your message and pitch to be remembered.

# Key Points

## Potent

*Ending Your Pitch with Power & Avoiding the Mistakes Other Speakers Make*

We all have a tendency to recall the first and last items with what is known as the Serial Position Effect.

The last words of a pitch are therefore just as important as the first.

Creating a closing that has an impact will ensure you and your pitch are remembered.

# CHAPTER 8

## Pitch Deck

### How to Create a Pitch Deck that Gets You the Desired Result

With all the information you have prepared, we can now create the slides to support your pitch.

The slide presentation you will design is commonly referred to as a pitch deck.

While it can be very tempting to want to share with a buyer or investor all the fascinating details that make your product or service so special and unique, it is a temptation that you will need to resist.

The information covered in the pitch will best serve you when it is at a level that gives an overview of your product or service.

Getting too in depth at this stage, in the short time you will have to deliver your pitch, will result in you losing everyone's interest and an opportunity.

If there is any part of the product or service that you have not covered that the buyer or investor is interested in hearing more details on, they will be able to ask you to provide these during the pitch.

## Slides for Your Pitch Deck

When you are pitching to an investor, there are 13 primary slides to include in your pitch deck.

These slides will provide the investor with all of the information they require to understand your business, ask pertinent questions and consider an investment.

When you are pitching to a buyer, you will only need to share with them the information contained on slides 1 to 5, plus 13.

## Slide 1: Title

The purpose of the title slide is to introduce both you and the product or service that is going to be offered to those attending the meeting at which you are pitching.

Include on this slide your name and that of your product/service or its slogan.

## Slide 2: Vision

This slide will state in a single short sentence, exactly what it is that you provide to all of your customers.

Create and display on the slide a single sentence or phrase that encapsulates your product or service.

An awareness of your business at this stage will help the attendees to be better placed to understand and follow along with the rest of your pitch.

## Slide 3: Problem

Now is the time to demonstrate and explain all the problems you see with the products or services that are currently available on the market.

It will help with the attendees' understanding if you are specific about the problems you believe exist with the current products or services.

Helping to raise attendees' awareness of the problems will allow them to appreciate your solution later in your pitch more easily.

## Slide 4: Market Opportunity

The buyer and investor will both be very keen to hear who you consider the specific target audience or customer for your product or service.

They will also like to hear from you the projected demand and market size.

Demonstrate exactly how you see your product or service fitting into the existing market.

To show the massive opportunity there is for the buyer or investor, it will seem reasonable to portray the market for your product or service to be as extensive as possible.

Inflating the market possibilities for your product or service will be detected and therefore likely to backfire.

Impress the buyer or investor by presenting specific and relevant statistics on the opportunity.

The figures will show them how you have researched and fully understand your market.

It will be crucial for you to know the basis for your statistics, being prepared to back them up with reputable sources when asked for them.

**Slide 5: Solution**

Here you will describe how you are best positioned to resolve the problem and issues raised in slide 3 with your product or service.

Explain or, even better, demonstrate how all of the potential customers will use the product.

If it is a physical product that is in production, hand it to the attendees so they can feel its quality or test its features.

Maybe you have a mock-up, drawings or a video to show your solution in action.

Include any customer feedback or testimonials that will help to corroborate this as an innovation that you are bringing to the market.

## Slide 6: Business Model

When you are pitching to investors, this part of your pitch will be critical to whether you are going to maintain their interest and receive any money.

The investors will need to know how you are going to generate sales and income from your product or service.

Investors will also be interested in hearing the cost of acquiring each customer and their average lifetime value to your business.

## Slide 7: Marketing Plan

Now is the time to outline how you are planning to grow your business with a defined sales and marketing strategy.

How are you going to get your customers' attention and grow your business?

Investors are aware how getting market attention for any product or service will be more demanding for a new company.

Display to the investor a defined strategy on your target market and the sales channels required.

**Slide 8: Management Team**

Investors would like to know there is a management team in place with the experience to guide the company and take care of their investment.

On this slide, show photographs of the individual members of your management team and their relevant experience and previous business or career successes.

If you have a vacancy in the team, identify it so the investor can see the positions you recognise as required to the success of the business.

## Slide 9: Financial Projections

In addition to your enthusiasm, ideas and vision, investors will need to see your financial projections for the next 3 years at a minimum.

Share with the investors your projections for any sales, profit, loss and cash flow over the 3-year period.

The investors will also be keen to see how and where you are planning to spend any money invested in your business.

The projections will need to be realistic and corroborate with each of the other figures presented in the pitch.

As you are going to be asked questions on the financial projections, be sure to know how they have been calculated, along with any of the underlying assumptions they contain.

## Slide 10: Competitive Analysis

Raising awareness of the competition is one area that entrepreneurs can feel uncomfortable mentioning during their pitch.

When you first think about it, why would you want to draw attention to your competitors?

There can be advantages to showing any competitors, as this demonstrates market strength and the profits they are achieving.

The competitors' strengths and weaknesses can be displayed along with how you are going to differentiate yourself in the market with the features, pricing or service provided.

If there honestly is no other company competing to offer the same service or product, the investor may wonder why and if there is any demand in the market for your product or service.

If there is no other company in the same space, show the solution your target market is currently using and how your product or service will now benefit them.

## Slide 11: Investment

Now is the time for you to deliver a call to action by asking for the investment required for your business.

The investors will need to know how much you are seeking, the type of funding and how exactly you are planning to use any investment to achieve the plans you have laid out in your pitch.

Whatever the investment will be used to achieve (tooling, design, marketing), be prepared to explain precisely how, when and where it will be used.

When you have received other investments into your business, it will be appropriate to disclose them here along with the amount and purpose.

**Slide 12: Exit**

When an investor receives equity in your business in exchange for their money, they will need to know how and when they will see a return.

The investor will receive a return when they can exit the business. The investor's exit from the business will usually occur in one of two ways.

Firstly, it is when the business has grown significantly to make it of interest to another company who buys it.

The second way for an investor to exit the business is when, after a period of growth, shares are listed and sold on the stock market.

Explain your plans to the investor on when they will be able to exit the business with a return on their money.

### Slide 13: Close

On this slide include details on how the buyer or investor can contact you.

The slide will need to have your name and that of the company. Provide a business address along with your contact email details and phone numbers.

## Supplying Slides

When pitching to investors, it is likely that they will ask for a copy of your presentation either in advance or after your pitch.

Unlike the other entrepreneurs who will frequently send over the original slides from the pitch, think of these as two separate documents.

When the investor reviews your presentation while sitting alone, what is the information the slides will convey to them without your explanation and enthusiasm?

## Appendices

When sending or supplying copies of your pitch book to the buyers or investors, take time to review the slides.

Look to see what details can be included or updated to share with the buyers or investors that will increase your chances of receiving their interest and investment.

The additional details you would like to include can be added as appendices to your pitch book.

For example, you may feel it will help to include in the appendices all the key assumptions underpinning your financial projections or your methodology to calculate the market size/opportunity.

**Formatting**

To help with the readability of your pitch book, you will want it to display as it was designed when viewed on any laptop, tablet or mobile device.

The safest way for you to be sure your pitch book does display as designed is to export or save it as a PDF.

.

# Key Points

## Pitch Deck

*How to Create a Pitch Deck that Gets You the Desired Result*

Maintain interest in your pitch by presenting the information as a high-level overview of your product or service.

There are 13 main slides to include in your pitch required for investors.

Use these slides to provide all of the essential information the investor requires on your business.

## Pitch Deck

When pitching to buyers, they will be less interested in your management team and financial arrangements.

When you receive a request for a copy of your pitch book, think of it as an additional document. Plan and prepare what further information you can include.

Take the time to export and send the document as a PDF.

# CHAPTER 9

## Presence

*Speaking with Presence, Delivering Your Pitch with Impact*

This is it!

The moment you have been preparing and practicing for is almost here.

You are about to deliver your pitch.

It is during these moments before you start your pitch where any nerves or tension that you may be feeling are likely to reach their peak.

These were the moments when I used to experience every single known symptom of public speaking nerves.

In this chapter, we will cover what to do in the moments before you speak and what to do in the first minute after you start.

Let me share with you some of the ways that have helped me to lose and reduce those feelings of extreme anxiety that I would always experience in the moments before speaking in public.

If you are going to be speaking in a large room, it is very likely that the seating is laid out in what is known as 'theatre style'.

This is the room layout you are most likely to be familiar with as all the chairs are in rows with a walkway that is usually down the middle.

When you are speaking in a large room, take the opportunity before you are introduced to stand up and walk to the back.

Taking the chance to move before speaking gives you the opportunity to loosen up and ensure your legs have not "gone to sleep".

Moving around will also help you to burn off any nervous energy which is all part of the process of getting ready for your pitch.

Ideally, take a seat towards the back of the room, so you do not draw any attention from those attending the meeting as you stand up in advance of your pitch.

When you are introduced as the next speaker, or it is your turn to speak, the slightly longer walk from the back of the room to the speaking area will give you another opportunity to use up some of the nervous energy, loosen up and focus your mind.

Standing up and moving around before speaking will not always be possible.

When you are delivering your pitch in a meeting with, say, an individual investor or perhaps a couple of buyers, standing up and moving around for a few minutes before speaking would look rather strange.

When you are speaking in this situation or would prefer not to walk to the back of the meeting room, there are still some steps you can take to stretch and loosen up.

Here is how to do it.

> Sit with both feet flat on the floor so that your legs are uncrossed.
>
> Slowly stretch one of your legs out so that it is straight and your foot is pointing forward.
>
> Hold it in this position for 2 seconds then, slowly draw it back towards you.
>
> Place your foot so that it is again flat on the floor.
>
> Now repeat the process for the other leg.

This leg stretching exercise will help you feel more relaxed and ready for your pitch, so ideally repeat it several times.

In any situation we feel some stress, this exercise is a covert way to stretch and loosen up without drawing any attention.

Even when we are not planning to deliver a pitch, there are times in our professional or personal lives where we can sometimes be asked to speak in public.

## Recalling My Own Name

While working in the corporate world and attending a training session or perhaps meetings with new teams, we would often be called upon to introduce ourselves.

The way it would usually work would be to go around the table saying our name and department.

My name and department were details that I naturally knew very well and without having to give them any thought.

However, the worry and stress of speaking in public would have me mentally reciting my name and department in which I worked while waiting for my turn to speak.

The result of mentally reciting my name and department over and over again while waiting my turn?

When we had finished the exercise, I still hardly knew the names of anyone sitting around the table.

My focus had been on getting my details correct, which meant I was unable to listen to any of my colleagues as they introduced themselves.

The only voice I heard was my own.

The stress of having to speak to the room would often even make talking difficult as I experienced all those same symptoms of speaking fears like butterflies in my stomach, racing heart, and a dry throat.

Have you ever been in this situation when just saying something simple like your name bought out some of those public speaking fears?

As these unthreatening situations led me to experience extreme anxiety, you can imagine how standing in front of a room would make me feel!

## Breathing Air into Our Pitch

When we start to feel stress, we naturally change the way we are breathing.

Without realising it, we start a breathing cycle that is fast and shallow.

This type of breathing cycle may once have been a life saver when we needed to run away from a lion; however, it will hinder us when we want to speak to deliver our pitch.

Here is a terrific technique that will help you to steady your nerves while regulating your breathing rate so you will begin to feel more relaxed.

Use the technique below anytime you feel stressed as it will help you to regulate your breathing, returning it to normal.

> Place both feet flat on the floor and relax your arms.
>
> Slowly and silently breathe in for 4 seconds.
>
> Hold your breath for 4 seconds.
> Slowly and silently breathe out for 4 seconds.
>
> Hold for 4 seconds.
>
> Slowly and silently breathe in for 4 seconds.

As you repeat this cycle of slow and regulated breathing, you will feel your body relaxing and all the stress slowly slipping away, helping you to feel calmer and confident.

The power of this technique is how it gets you to breathe deeply and slowly.

Undertake this exercise anytime you are feeling some stress without anyone ever noticing or realising what you are doing.

## 4 Square Breathing

The '4 Square' breathing exercise is one that I have taught to a wide variety of business people who hold positions ranging from international directors to interns, all of whom have found it immensely powerful in times of stress, so I know it will work for you.

If you are standing up at the back of a room as mentioned earlier in this chapter, this is an exercise to complete as you are waiting to walk towards the speaking area.

Stand with your back straight, head up and looking forward with your arms hanging loosely at your sides while completing the breathing cycles.

## The Big Moment

Let us cover how you can start off your pitch in a way that will let everyone know you have arrived and that it is now time to pay attention.

### Approach

To guarantee you appear confident and in control when it comes to the moment for you to enter the speaking area where you will stand while delivering your pitch, walk forward with purpose and at a steady pace, but without rushing.

In the past, with the adrenaline pumping, I have often made the mistake of jumping up from my seat and rushing to the front of the room as though there was some emergency or an announcement that I had to deliver urgently.

Standing up in front of people short of breath from rushing was always a poor way for me to start my pitches.

You will want those attending the meeting to have confidence in you and what you are about to say. One way to do this is to look in control of both yourself and the situation, so take your time.

**Position**

In the speaking area, move to stand in the spot central to your listeners. This spot may be the middle of the table or even in line with a central walkway if speaking in a larger room with the chairs set up in theatre style.

The walkway between the rows of chairs may not be central to the audience.

For example, the room may have been laid out with rows of 10 chairs on the left and 7 on the right.

In this case, standing to face the walkway will not be central to your audience.

**Addressing the Audience**

When standing in the speaking area, one sure sign of nervousness is when the speaker stands too far away from their audience.

The distance that is appropriate for you to stand away from the front row or table will vary on the occasion, room size and how well you know the people attending.

If you are there to present in a meeting room with 2 people attending, it will be best for you to stand much closer to them than if there were 200 attendees in an auditorium.

Be aware of where you are standing, as there is a natural temptation when feeling nervous to edge backwards away from the listeners.

There have been many times when the only reason for me not to have stepped further back was the wall pressing against me!

Standing too far back sends a signal that you are feeling nervous and creates some disengagement with the people at the meeting.

When you stand close to your listeners, you will appear confident and in control, even if you are not particularly feeling it at the time.

While it is natural to feel some nerves, we will want to appear confident in the business, product or service we are there to pitch.

## Stance

As you arrive in the speaking area, do not say a single word!

Yep, that is right, stay silent.

All too often, speakers will start to deliver their pitch immediately they stand up or reach the front of the room and even before they have turned to face those keenly waiting to hear from them.

Speaking before turning around results in a poor initial impression as the opening few words will be directed towards the back wall and easily missed by those attending.

As you stand in a central position, close to your listeners and facing them, rather than speaking, take the opportunity to adjust your stance and settle in to 'claim' the speaking area.

# Presence

Stand squarely with your back straight, head up and with your arms hanging naturally and relaxed at your side.

Now take a deep, slow and silent breath.

Breathing is obviously a required part of our lives, yet we somehow forget to do it properly when first facing the people waiting to hear our pitch.

Smile as you look around at the people attending the meeting.

Starting your pitch with a warm, genuine smile will be appreciated and reciprocated by the people attending.

We usually smile back at people when they smile at us, which contributes to creating a friendly environment.

The whole process of arriving in the speaking area, moving into the best position, adjusting your stance, taking a breath while smiling and looking out at the meeting attendees will take just a few seconds to complete.

These few seconds will prove to have a positive impact on how you feel at the start of your pitch and how those attending the meeting feel about you.

Now is the time to start your pitch.

## Avoid This

Whenever a speaker is feeling anxious, nervous or under pressure while presenting, they will often start to undermine their own credibility and authority on the subject about which they are going to speak.

The speaker will know the opening of their pitch, but for some reason go suddenly off script.

Instead of delivering the opening to their pitch that they have prepared and practiced, they start making excuses.

They feel that if they make excuses, everyone will be more forgiving and understanding of any mistakes they make.

Making excuses is what I used to believe was the best way to start my pitch to have a sympathetic audience.

The reality is the buyers or investors start to wonder why they are wasting their time.

As covered earlier in this book, you only have a few sentences to make an impact, so do not waste them with excuses.

Some of the opening sentences made by speakers that undermine their credibility and authority are ones like these: -

Unfortunately.

I'm a bit stressed.

I'm feeling really nervous.

I've had some computer issues.

I'm not used to speaking in public.

I didn't have much time to prepare.

A few things might go wrong today.

I know you can't read this (the pitch slide).

When speakers start making excuses like these, they will be the only ones to feel slightly better.

You have prepared your pitch, you have practiced, you are ready to present.

Present!

Deliver only your prepared opening sentences, rather than excuses that undermine your credibility to be pitching.

## Eye Contact

Your eyes are a powerful tool to help you connect and engage with the attendees.

While we are having a one-to-one conversation with a friend or colleague, we would not avoid making any eye contact.

If we did, they would start to think that we were hiding something from them or being untruthful.

The same applies when we are speaking to other business professionals or during our pitch.

Speaking nerves used to have me looking either over everyone's heads, at the floor or even the ceiling.

While doing so for a few seconds will not be noticed, doing so for extended periods will create a disconnect with everyone attending the meeting.

Making eye contact creates a connection with the people attending the meeting as they will feel included and part of your pitch.

You will only need to look at a person or area for a few seconds before slowly looking at someone else in another area of the room.

Making the change in eye contact slow and purposeful will help to ensure you do not appear to be watching a tennis match with rapid movement from side to side.

## Letting Go of My Blanket

Whenever I used to hold any notes during a pitch or presentation, I would find myself continually looking down and referring to them, even though I knew the content and what I would be covering.

Why did I keep referring to my notes if I knew the content?

The speaker notes were acting as my 'security blanket'.

Repeatedly looking at my notes may have reassured me everything was going well and to plan.

That my pitch was on schedule with everything being covered as I had prepared.

However, repeatedly looking at my notes was breaking the connection that I was trying to establish with those listening to me.

Do you like to use notes when delivering your pitch? If you like to prepare notes for when you are delivering your pitch, create them on small index cards rather than on sheets of paper.

Small cards make finding your place a lot quicker, allowing you to look back up and at those attending the meeting.

There is one important reason you will want to look at everyone attending.

It will allow you to see how they are reacting to your pitch.

>   Do they look bored?
>   Do they look confused?
>   Do they look interested?
>   Are they all following you?

As you read the audience and gauge their reaction, you can then adjust your pitch.

# **Key Points**

## Presence

*Speaking with Presence, Delivering Your Pitch with Impact*

To relieve stress when a pitch is being delivered in a larger room, move to the back to loosen up and focus your mind.

If sitting in a small meeting, stretching your legs will help you prepare.

Calm any nerves, stress or anxiety you may feel with the 4 Square breathing exercise.

When it comes to your moment to speak, stand and without rushing, walk forward with purpose and at a steady pace.

Settle into the speaking area before starting your pitch.

Avoid undermining your own credibility by sticking to the script.

Look at the people attending the meeting, making purposeful eye contact.

# CHAPTER 10

# P.R.O.M.P.T Presentations™

*Speaking On The Spot With Confidence*

Throughout our lives, those around us like family, friends and colleagues are continually asking us questions as they seek out new or additional information from us.

These are most likely to be the usual day to day questions like what time is lunch? where is the stapler? or, in what room is the meeting taking place?

We can usually give them an instant reply without a second thought, readily supplying them with the information they sought from us.

Then there are the more challenging questions our colleagues or clients ask us that we are still able to answer, even when we do not have all the information to hand.

We can even answer these questions in some way when we are unsure of the details.

When we are placed in a more formal setting and asked even the simplest of questions, our brains seem to 'freeze' as a feeling of sudden stress starts to set in.

In years gone by, while sitting happily in a meeting, when someone suddenly asked me a question, I would struggle to answer.

The reply to their question would start with something like: -

*"er... cough... erm... I... cough... er..."*

Starting my sentences with errs and erms was something that I would never do when asked questions outside of the meeting, even when struggling to find the answer.

Once I had finished giving my answer and starting to feel calmer, I would always be able to think of all the other points that I should have included.

Why is that?

When put on the spot, especially when it is entirely unexpected, the sudden surge of adrenaline and cortisol makes it almost impossible to process the information and create a clear reply.

The temptation is to say something immediately, anything!

That is when we start making all those err and erm sounds to fill the silence.

With the process you are about to learn in this chapter, never again will this happen to you.
You will now be able to clearly and concisely answer any question asked.

While questions may be posed to you at any time, they certainly will during the meeting at which you are delivering your pitch.

The Question and Answer (Q&A) section of a pitch was the one area that used to cause me the most concern.

Incorrectly, I felt the Q&A part of a pitch was something that could not be prepared for in advance, or any of the questions predicted.

As you will have seen earlier in this book, the advanced research required before creating your pitch will prepare you for answering all of the questions likely to be asked.

When it comes to taking questions, the answers you give to the buyer or investor should be considered a mini-presentation.

Each answer delivered as a logically connected and consistent response to what may be a probing question.

This is where P.R.O.M.P.T Presentations™ will always help you. A proven proprietary process to position you as an informed and competent professional.

Let us explore how you can deliver P.R.O.M.P.T Presentations™ even when faced with the most probing or provocative questions.

**Pause**

As we now know, the sudden surge of adrenaline and cortisol makes us want to start speaking immediately the question is asked.

Even sometimes before the person asking the question has finished speaking.

We can then end up even talking over them while delivering what ends up as a poorly structured reply. The first step when creating your P.R.O.M.P.T presentation is to pause.

Pausing may seem obvious, yet is the one thing professionals do not do when suddenly put on the spot.

There is no 'law' or requirement that says you must start to speak literally at the very second the other person has finished asking their question, so pause.

This pause will only need to be for a couple of seconds, during which it will provide valuable time to process the full point of what you have been asked and to start formulating an answer.

We can sometimes be conscious of silence and feel we need to fill them by saying something.

Yet these couple of seconds will not even be noticed by those attending the meeting.

If you happen to take a few extra seconds, they will think that you are giving a considered answer to the question which helps to build your credibility.

It always amazes me how our brains can process the information it receives so quickly.

By briefly pausing, we are giving our brains an additional second or two which will help with formulating the answer.

## Relax

The second component of delivering a P.R.O.M.P.T presentation is to take a moment to relax.

When you find yourself in the spotlight and being asked to answer a question, it is natural to feel some stress.

If you think the person asking the question is challenging you in some way, then it is likely to increase the feelings of stress in this situation.

In these circumstances, it is vital to take a moment to relax and reduce any stress you may be feeling.

There is an easy and efficient way to start reducing the symptoms of stress. Take a single, slow, silent breath before you start delivering the answer to the question.

We will often take shallow, rapid breaths when feeling stressed that do not provide us with the oxygen required for the situation we are facing.

Taking a single, slow, silent breath will have incredible benefits in helping to reduce any symptoms of stress you are feeling at the time.

Breathing this way is a good practice to incorporate in the pause you take before speaking as described in the previous section.

Keep the breath silent so that it will not be perceived as showing any level of frustration or impatience with the question.

## **Observe**

Many years ago, I recall how during one particular meeting, I spent a full two minutes giving my answer to a complicated technical question before it dawned on me that this was not what they had asked me.

When placed on the spot and under stress, it is tempting to rush into answering the question we thought we had been asked as I did in the meeting, rather than the actual one posed.

There can be a temptation to latch onto the first part of the question and start formulating an answer.

While we are doing this, we close out the rest of what the other person is saying which may contain the real question that they are asking.

If you have any doubt as to the question, ask for them to repeat it. You may also choose to repeat the question back to check your understanding is correct.

Avoid the temptation of adopting this strategy for every question during a Q&A session or interview as a way to delay delivering your answer and gain extra time while you formulate a response.

Asking for every question to be repeated will soon start to seem evasive by those attending.

When following the two previous stages of the P.R.O.M.P.T Presentations process of pausing before answering the question and relaxing by taking a full breath, use this time to observe the question.

Following this process will guarantee you are now able to answer and address the question asked.

## **Muted**

We can sometimes find ourselves being asked questions that are deliberately antagonistic, challenging or provocative in nature.

When faced with answering these types of questions, it will be important to maintain your professionalism and remain in control.

If you start giving an uncertain or rambling answer, it will show that you have been caught off guard or are on the defensive.

This will be perceived as a deficiency in your knowledge or competence.

There is something even worse that I have witnessed speakers do when in these situations. It is something you must always avoid.

You will never want to give into the temptation, or possibly even trap, of immediately hitting back with any form of retaliation or disparaging comment.

These may be made in the form of sarcasm, a dismissive remark or even trying to belittle the person who asked the question.

When finding yourself in these kinds of situations, it is important to stay muted or silent until you have formulated a considered, balanced reply.

Staying muted for just a few seconds is all it takes for your brain to create the appropriate sentences to start your considered answer to the challenging question that you have been asked.

The person asking the question is likely to know if they are being deliberately antagonistic, challenging or provocative, as will anyone else attending the meeting.

When people see you taking the time to consider your answer and responding in a controlled, considered way, you will look self-assured and convinced of the content both of your presentation and the answer.

This will strengthen the other attendees' confidence in your abilities and knowledge and maybe also that of the person asking the question.

## Précis

As you reach the end of delivering your answer to the question, it will add clarity and conviction if you give a précis of your main points.

If the answer you gave was extended or technical in nature, the précis will help those listening to recall and remember the points that you have made.

Be sure to pick out what are the essential points, rather than repeating the answer you gave.

A précis works best when it is kept short in relation to the time taken to give your full answer.

Including a précis with your reply is a potent tool for showing your status as a confident, competent, communicator.

## **Transition**

When you reach the end of your answer and précis, it will be time to transition back to the person who asked you the question.

Creating a seamless transition is an essential component of delivering an answer that professionals will often neglect to include.

Many business people I have seen will deliver a well-structured answer, then not know how to transition back to the person who asked the question.

They may simply say something like: -

'...well...that is all I have really got to say...'

The transition you use will depend on the situation you are in and the answer that you have given.

You may say something like: -

> "Does that answer your question?"

or

> "That is why I believe (repeat key point)".

Finish your answers with a transition that is positive and confident.

The P.R.O.M.P.T Presentations™ process is a very powerful way to create and deliver compelling answers to questions when put on the spot, in what are usually stressful situations for us.

# Key Points

## P.R.O.M.P.T Presentations™

*Speaking On The Spot With Confidence*

Take your time to answer when put on the spot.

Avoid the temptation to jump in immediately with an answer.

Breathe slowly and silently to help reduce your stress.

Ensure the question you have heard is the one asked.

Finish your answer confidently.

# CHAPTER 11

## Probe

*Dealing With Questions*

*How You Can Answer Questions With Confidence*

The Question and Answer (Q&A) session can bring its own unique set of challenges for you to overcome, ensuring you present yourself positively and achieve the purpose of your pitch.

When you are at a meeting pitching for an order or investment, the people attending will think of you as the subject matter expert, so able to answer all of the questions they may have on your business, product and service.

## What Questions?

As part of your preparation, give thought to all of the questions you are likely to be asked on the subject of your pitch.

The questions you think of will help to fill any gaps in your subject knowledge, especially if this is a colleague's area of expertise.

An approach that has worked well for me is to think of what questions I would want to ask if it was me sitting and listening to the pitch.

## Who will Answer?

If you are delivering the pitch with another person, decide in advance your arrangements for the Q&A session.

The pitch professionalism can start to quickly unravel if you talk over each other or, even worse, disagree in public.

Agree in advance who will take the lead in answering questions from the attendees.

## Sensible or Pointless?

There are times when you may be asked a question that you consider pointless, obvious or maybe off subject.

When receiving these types of questions, proceed to answer them as you would any other, treating the person asking with full respect and gratitude for raising the point with you.

Maintaining your professionalism as you listen and respond to the question will contribute to your status and standing with everyone else who is attending the meeting.

## Sharing the Questions

You will notice in larger meetings, the people sitting close to the front will usually speak quieter than those seated towards the back when they are asking questions, as they know you will be able to hear them.

People sitting further back may have been unable to hear the question asked, so you may need to repeat it before starting your answer.

Repeating the question will help to ensure everyone can understand the context of your answer and the points made in reply.

When you are repeating the question, ideally include the name of the person who asked.

You may do this by saying something like 'Maureen asked…'.

Including the person's name will let everyone in the audience know who it was that asked the question.

An added benefit of saying who asked the question is that it will help to make the person feel valued and their contribution appreciated.

## Hearing the Questions

There will be times during your Q&A session when you are asked a question that you will not have heard clearly.

This may be due to noise in or outside of the room or perhaps the person asking the question spoke quietly.

When you have been unable to hear a question, immediately be honest and say so straight away, asking for the question to be repeated.

As the person asking is seeking some information from you, they will be happy to help you by repeating their question.

## Repeating to Delay

In Q&A sessions, I have often seen speakers asking for every one of the questions to be repeated.

After a while, the people attending the meeting start to see this as a way for the speaker to delay answering the questions.

If you have genuinely not heard the question, do ask for it to be repeated before starting to answer.

When you have heard the question, pause for a second and then start to deliver your reply using the methods contained in this book.

## Rephrasing For Clarity

Occasionally you will find that you do not understand a question, even after the person has repeated it.

When this happens, be up-front with the person who has asked you the question, requesting they rephrase it to help you.

The person asking will usually take this as an opportunity to expand on their original question, providing you with additional valuable information that will help with your answer.

## Prepping Your Answer

Once you are sure of the question asked, you will want to deliver a clear, concise and confident reply.

You will find using a framework will help you to create and deliver a structured answer.

One of the best frameworks used to create an organised answer is known as P.R.E.P.

The P.R.E.P framework stands for: -

*Point* – Your opinion, reason or belief in response to the question asked.

*Reason* – Share the reason for your point of view.

*Example* – Now give an example that supports your reason and point of view.

*Point* – Conclude by summarising your main point and checking back with the person who asked the question.

P.R.E.P is a powerful framework to follow when answering questions in a professional environment.

## Starting Sensibly

When attending meetings and listening to speakers answer questions, you can often hear them start their sentence with a phrase similar to 'that's a good question'.

It may well have been a good question, however, when this phrase is repeatedly used as their standard first sentence, it provides little value or endorsement to the person asking.

When the speaker later misses this phrase out as their starting sentence, does it then mean that particular person has not asked a good question?

As every question is valid, the answer is yes it was a good question. That, however, may not be how the person asking the question may feel.

When answering questions, you will be seen as more honest and authentic when you deliver a thoughtful reply to address the point that has been raised.

## Eye Contact

As children, we are taught that it is polite to look at people when we are speaking to them.

This belief continues in meetings where speakers will often only look at the person who asked the question when answering.

When the answer is anything but brief, it can soon start to seem we are watching a private conversation.

We all like to feel included, so take the time to look around the room as this will keep everyone interested.

## Probe

The following steps will help you to ensure everyone attending the meeting feels included while you are answering questions.

> As you start delivering your reply, initially look at the person who asked the question.
>
> After a few sentences, slowly start to move your eyes to look at the other people attending, looking at everyone while delivering your reply.
>
> When reaching the end of your answer, bring your focus back to the person who asked you the question.

## When You Do Not Know The Answer

One of the biggest worries with Q&A sessions is that a question could be asked to which you do not know the answer.

What can you do in these situations?

The one thing to avoid doing is pretending you know the answer and making something up. Pretending you know can become even more challenging if there are then some follow-up questions.

If the buyers or investors feel you are either trying to avoid answering their question or even worse, deceive them, the whole pitch can soon start to fall apart, along with the loss of confidence they had in you.

Once any buyer or investor has concluded the person pitching is trying to deceive them, there is no chance of a successful conclusion to the meeting.

When asked a question which you are unable to answer, the person asking will appreciate it if you are honest and say you will need to find out the information.

Follow this by giving a firm commitment to communicate the answer to the person who asked the question and anyone else who would like to receive it.

Let them know precisely when they will receive the answer to their question, such as by 4pm today.

## Ask a Colleague

There may be times when you feel a colleague attending the pitch meeting would be better placed to provide an answer to a question.

In these circumstances, you can invite them to take the question.

To save any potential awkwardness, you would only want to ask your colleague when convinced they will know all of the details requested.

Only asking a colleague you know has the details will save you from giving any appearance of trying to dodge the question or divert attention.

When inviting a colleague who you know will be able to answer the question, say their name as you invite them to answer in case their attention happens to be focused somewhere else.

After inviting your colleague to answer, repeat the question as they may have missed it being asked.

An example of how to invite a colleague to take the question is: -

> 'Jo, Teresa has asked if we have any regulatory risks. Would you be able to provide the details?'

## Aggressive Questions

As we covered in an earlier chapter, there may be the occasional situation where you are going to be faced with having to answer questions that are intended to be antagonistic, challenging or provocative in nature.

There is a difference between a person asking questions you are less keen to answer, such as when they are trying to drill into your company finances, and someone who is being deliberately antagonistic, challenging or provocative in the questions they are asking.

If you should ever happen to find yourself in this situation, it is imperative to maintain your composure and dignity.

When you are seen to be staying calm and courteous throughout the exchange, you will keep the support and respect of those attending and even the person asking.

Retaining your composure will also allow you to think more clearly and able to deal with the questioner.

## Repetitive Questions

There are likely to be times when you feel the people listening to your pitch, just are not getting 'it'.

All of the questions you are asked are on areas you consider having been clearly covered in your pitch.

While you may feel these areas were adequately explained, take a note of the questions that have been asked.

This list of questions can later be reviewed and incorporated into your pitch prior to the next meeting.

## Asking The Wrong Question

You may be asked a question or have someone make a point that you feel is incorrect during your pitch.

It will help you to keep the person asking or making the point on side if your reply does not start with a phrase that is often used in these situations: -

"no, that's wrong...".

Starting with this type of response can easily provoke the person asking the question to enter into an extended debate with you on the issue they raised.

Even if they remain silent, they could be left feeling either annoyed or embarrassed.

These are situations that you will want to avoid when the purpose of the pitch is to receive an order or investment from them.

When starting your answer, rather than saying "no, that is wrong...", look for less direct ways to start your reply.

A subtler way to reply could be to say: -

> *My feeling is...*
>
> *The general view is...*
>
> *Other people feel...*
>
> *My clients believe...*

Having subtly started your sentence, share your thoughts on the question or point they made.

This approach will keep your potential buyer or investor onside and open to hearing your response.

# Key Points

## Probe

*Dealing With Questions*

*How You Can Answer Questions With Confidence*

Give thought to all of the questions you are likely to be asked as part of your preparation.

When delivering the pitch with a colleague, agree in advance who will take the lead in answering questions.

Even if you feel a question is pointless or off subject, maintain your professionalism and treat the person asking with full respect.

Repeat a question if required to ensure everyone heard it and will know the context of your reply.

Ask for a question to be repeated if you were unable to hear it being asked.

If you are unable to understand a question, ask for it to be rephrased.

Use the P.R.E.P framework to create an organised, structured answer.

Seek to avoid starting replies to questions with the same phrase such as 'that's a good question'.

Help everyone in the meeting to feel included by making eye contact with them.

When you do not know the answer to a question, be honest and tell them. Provide a firm commitment to communicate the answer by a set day and time.

## Probe

If faced with hostile or aggressive questions, maintain your composure and dignity to keep everyone's support.

Making a note of the questions asked will help you to improve the pitch ready for the next meeting.

When you feel the question asked or a point made is incorrect, rather than saying "no, that is wrong", start with a less direct sentence to keep your potential buyer or investor onside.

# ABOUT
# ANDY O'SULLIVAN

*How to Achieve Success in The Business World*

In his books, workshops and seminars, Andy teaches professionals how to dramatically increase their rise up the corporate career ladder and grow their business by creating and presenting presentations that inspire, impress and ensure they are the obvious choice.

Andy enjoyed a successful corporate career that saw him working for many of the leading financial institutions and international banks.

It was while working in the corporate world that Andy recognised the need to develop his own public speaking and presentation skills.

A long and, at times, painful journey that led him to develop the renowned Corporate Confidence System™.

The Corporate Confidence System™ utilises all of Andy's knowledge and extensive experience from the real world, so professionals are now able to swiftly create speeches that connect with clients, colleagues and even the CEO.

The incredible success of the Corporate Confidence System™ and constant demand by entrepreneurs and startup founders for Andy to share his extensive experience with them, led to the development of the now acclaimed Startup Success System™.

A system that ensures entrepreneurs and startup founders are able to create pitches that will impress their important investors and buyers, winning them that crucial investment or order.

## About Andy O'Sullivan

The commitment Andy has continually shown in helping people to learn effective public speaking and presentation skills has been recognised by all the international awards and accolades he has received.

Andy is the founder of the Academy of Public Speakers, a leading provider of public speaking and presentation skills training.

You can contact Andy directly at: -

Andy@academyofpublicspeakers.com
www.academyofpublicspeakers.com
**LinkedIn:** - http://andy.chat/linkedin
**Twitter:** - http://andy.chat/Twitter
**Facebook:** - http://andy.chat/facebook

# Acknowledgments

I will never be able to express enough thanks to my Mum for her never-ending love and support. Standing by me and always being there throughout the bad times as well as the good.

To my sister Maureen for her love, patience and fantastic assistance with this book.

To my sister Teresa for those early lessons in English.

To my brother Peter for being my willing and original chauffeur.

Thanks to Tanvir Arafat for providing the inspiration to write a book that would help fellow entrepreneurs to achieve success and for his continued encouragement and endless positive energy.

To Hien Vo. Always working long hours and very busy, yet will still make the time to give me his support, guidance, encouragement and treasured friendship.

Thanks to Naynesh Patel for giving me a helping hand whenever I asked and even when I didn't.

To Jagdeep Sidhu for his 16 years of precious friendship and loyalty.

Thanks to Michael Wright for his loyalty, friendship and for standing by me all through those tough times.

To Paul Gridley for his support and advice on the crucial matters of the day.

Thanks to Michael for working so hard to give us all that he possibly could.

# Acknowledgments

To Ralph C. Smedley, without whom my journey of self-development and growth would have been so much longer and harder.

A final word of gratitude to all those who have guided and supported me during my long and, at times, painful journey.

# References

Covey, S. (2004). The 7 habits of highly effective people. London: Simon & Schuster.

Rodionova, Zlata. "The 12 Words To Say In An Interview That Can Land (Or Lose) You The Job". The Independent. N.p., 2016. Web. 1 Apr. 2016.

"Serial Position Effect ". Indiana.edu. N.p., 2016. Web. 1 Apr. 2016.

"Presentation - Definition Of Presentation In English From The Oxford Dictionary". Oxforddictionaries.com. N.p., 2016. Web. 1 Apr. 2016.

"Pitch - Definition Of Pitch In English From The Oxford Dictionary". Oxforddictionaries.com. N.p., 2016. Web. 1 Apr. 2016.

"7 Shocking Health Statistics". Realbuzz 4. N.p., 2012. Web. 1 Apr. 2016.

# Bibliography

Avery, Matt. Successful Public Speaking In A Week. London: Teach Yourself, 2013. Print.

Beebe, Steven, and Beebe, Susan. Public Speaking, An Audience-Centered Approach. Mass.: Pearson, 2013. Print.

Bplans Blog. (2017). The 11 Slides You Need to Have in Your Pitch Deck - Bplans Blog. [online] Available at: https://articles.bplans.com/what-to-include-in-your-pitch-deck/ [Accessed 29 Dec. 2017].

Bplans Blog. (2017). What Startups Need to Know About Exit Strategies - Bplans Blog. [online] Available at: https://articles.bplans.com/what-startups-need-to-know-about-exit-strategies/ [Accessed 29 Dec. 2017].

Eldin, Peter et al. Speechmakers' Bible. London: Cassell Illustrated, 2006. Print.

Fripp, Patricia and LaCroix. Create Your Keynote By Next Week. USA: DVD.

Godefroy, Christian H, Stephanie Barrat-Godefroy, and Christian Godefroy. Confident Public Speaking. London: Piatkus, 1998. Print.

Jeffreys, Michael. Success Secrets Of The Motivational Superstars. Rocklin, CA: Prima Pub., 1996. Print.

Ledden, Emma. The Presentation Book. Harlow: Pearson, 2013. Print.

Linver, Sandy, and Jim Mengert. Speak And Get Results. New York: Simon & Schuster, 1994. Print.

Lucas, Stephen. The Art Of Public Speaking. Boston: McGraw-Hill Higher Education, 2009. Print.

Mueck, Florian. The Seven Minute Star. [North Charleston, S.C.]: [Createspace], 2010. Print.

Valentine, Craig, and Mitch Meyerson. World Class Speaking In Action. New York: Morgan James, 2015 Print.

Weissman, Jerry, and Jerry Weissman. Successful Presentation Strategies. Upper Saddle, New Jersey: FT Press, 2013. Print.

Yazbeck, Joe. No Fear Speaking. Odessa, FL: Paradies Publishing Co., 2014. Print.

Manufactured by Amazon.ca
Bolton, ON